Resources for
group time

Support for struggling readers

'Mr Gumpy's Outing'

& other texts

Level 1/2 activities
for 7–9 year olds

Kate Grant

Author Kate Grant
Editor Clare Gallaher
Assistant editor Roanne Davis
Series designers Paul Cheshire and Joy Monkhouse
Designer Martin Ford
Illustrations Mary Hall

Designed using Adobe Pagemaker
Published by Scholastic Ltd, Villiers House, Clarendon Avenue, Leamington Spa, Warwickshire CV32 5PR
Printed by Alden Group Ltd, Oxford
Text © Kate Grant
© 2001 Scholastic Ltd
1 2 3 4 5 6 7 8 9 0   1 2 3 4 5 6 7 8 9 0

British Library Cataloguing-in-Publication Data
A catalogue record for this book is available from the British Library.
ISBN 0-439-01947-8

Acknowledgements
The publishers gratefully acknowledge permission to reproduce the following copyright material:

● **The Random House Group Ltd** for the use of a scanned front cover, text and permission to base activities on the book *Mr Gumpy's Outing* by John Burningham © 1973, John Burningham (1973, Jonathan Cape) and for the use of the cover and for basing activities on *Titch* by Pat Hutchins © 1971, Pat Hutchins (1971, The Macmillan Company, USA).

● **Walker Books Ltd** for the use of a scanned front cover and permission to base activities on the book *The Pig in the Pond* by Martin Waddell © 1992, Martin Waddell (1992, Walker Books Ltd, London) and the use of illustrations and text and permission to base activities on the book of *Guess What I'll Be*, words by Louise Jackson and Paul Harrison, Text © 1998, Walker Books Ltd, Illustrations © 1998, Anni Axworthy (1998, Walker Books Ltd, London).

Every effort has been made to trace copyright holders for the works reproduced in this book and the publishers apologise for any inadvertent omissions.

Contents

Introduction

Why do I need resources for group time?

The National Literacy Strategy *Framework for Teaching* requires that all children's needs are catered for in the daily Literacy Hour. The class teacher can address individual needs through targeted questions and direct teaching in the first part of the hour when the whole class is taught. However, there is a real necessity for purposeful activities for those children who are struggling readers during the group/independent work section of the hour, when the teacher is working elsewhere with guided reading/writing groups. This book is designed to be used in Key Stage 2 classes, by a classroom assistant or other adult working with a group of children who are reading at Level 1–2.

How does the book work?

Each of the chapters in this book contains five photocopiable lessons, designed to fit into the 20-minute group/independent work slot in the Literacy Hour and to be used by a classroom assistant or other additional adult. The lessons are based on specific texts and children working on the activities will need to have access to them. The three story books are texts at Level 1 (Book Band 5–7):
* *Mr Gumpy's Outing* by John Burningham (Puffin)
* *Titch* by Pat Hutchins (Red Fox)
* *The Pig in the Pond* by Martin Waddell and Jill Barton (Walker Books).

The children do not need to be familiar with the text beforehand, as the classroom assistant will introduce the story and follow it with a shared reading activity in the lesson for Day 1.

Two non-fiction texts and poems (at Level 1–2) are provided as photocopiable pages. One story or extract is the focus for each week's lesson; the activities are at text, sentence and word level and include writing frames and homework tasks. The homework sheets could also be used independently by the children in class as revision and consolidation.

How does it fit into the Literacy Hour planning?

The learning objectives are chosen from earlier years of the framework, as recommended for pupils working at a lower level than the rest of the class. In most cases, the genre for a particular text will be found in the range for Years 3 or 4, for example stories in familiar settings, stories by significant children's authors, instructions, information texts on topics of interest, poems based on common themes. This makes it possible for struggling readers to be included more effectively in the Literacy Hour. The objectives are clearly indicated in the grid at the start of each chapter, allowing for simple group target-setting.

How flexible is it?

Each chapter in this book can be used independently – there is no need to follow any particular order. Although aimed at groups of children in Years 3 and 4, the activities could also be used with older children who have special needs, and are easily adapted for use with an individual child. The 20-minute format makes the activities ideal for the Literacy Hour, but they could equally be used at other times, for additional support.

Will classroom assistants need any training to use the book?

Everything that is needed to carry out the group-time lesson is explained in the straightforward notes for each day. There are also useful hints provided in the next few pages to help classroom assistants support children with reading, writing and spelling.

What is the range of the texts?

The three Level 1 fiction texts all fit the genres of stories with predictable and patterned language and stories by significant children's authors. *Titch* could also be used as a story with a familiar setting. Non-fiction texts are *Guess What I'll Be* and 'How to look after guinea pigs'. Poetry texts are traditional rhymes.

What objectives are covered?

Learning objectives include:
* **Text level:** predicting content, comprehension, sequencing, story writing, key words, reading and writing non-fiction, rhyme and rhythm
* **Sentence level:** capital letters, speech marks, word order, exclamation marks, punctuation in reading, questions
* **Word level:** spelling by analogy, high-frequency words, initial phonemes, word endings, long vowels, consonant clusters, new vocabulary, syllables.

High-frequency words/spelling by analogy

The following lists show the high-frequency words (from the National Literacy Strategy lists for Reception and Years 1 to 2) and spelling patterns (relating to phonics and spelling work for Years 1 to 2) that can be focused on when you are using the activities for each text.

	High-frequency words	Spelling patterns
Mr Gumpy's Outing	said	-oat
Titch	little	-ig
The Pig in the Pond	went	-un
Traditional rhymes	one	-et
Guess What I'll Be?	will	-ill
How to look after guinea pigs	look	-ook

Resources

A Big Book is useful for the introduction and shared reading of the fiction texts, but individual books could be used. A dry-wipe board or flip chart large enough to use with a group is an invaluable resource.

Reading

Before choosing a week's lessons, make sure the text being used is at an appropriate reading level (most children in the group should be able to read it with no more than one error in every ten words).

Children who are struggling readers in Key Stage 2 classes require support in their journey to independent reading. This can be thought of as providing a scaffold which is removed one piece at a time until they are confident to try reading a text by themselves.

Introducing the text: Clear guidance is provided in each chapter for introducing individual texts. At this stage, the children are familiarised with the story and encouraged to find a few key words.

Shared reading: At the second stage of the process, children join in with as much of the text as they are able, particularly any predictable and repeated phrases.

Independent reading: Finally, children tackle the text independently, often with the support of another child.

Consolidating reading skills: Day 2 always includes a re-reading of the now familiar text. It is easier for struggling readers to develop fluent and expressive reading on familiar texts.

Helping children with reading

Ask the children to tell you how they can work out a word they are finding difficult to read. They could:

- go back to the beginning of the sentence
- say the first sound and think of a word that fits
- leave out the difficult word, read a few more words, then have another try
- look for a little word they know inside the difficult word, for example *grandad*
- look for a pattern they know, for example *old* in *t**old***

  Remind the children of things they should ask themselves as they are reading:
- Does it make sense?
- Does it sound right?
- Does it look right?

Helping children with writing

The aim should be to enable the children to write as much as possible on their own, and your help will be geared to developing their skills. The writing frames provided in this book give the children a useful support, so that they are not faced with a blank sheet of paper. Discussion before writing is very important, as struggling readers usually have great difficulty in making the leap between thinking and expressing their thought in writing.

If children ask you how to spell a common (or high-frequency) word that they will need to use again in their writing, teach them to spell it by getting them to write it a few times using the Look–Say–Cover–Write–Check method (see page 6).

Another way to help is to draw boxes for the letters in the word, if it is one that can be 'sounded out' fairly easily. Ask what they can hear at the beginning, middle and end of the word, then help them to fill in the missing letters. For example, if a child wants to write *rocket,* ask him or her to say the word. Any letter sounds the child can hear (typically the *r, k* and *t*) can be written in the correct boxes.

Next, help the child to say the word again, emphasising each sound so that he or she can hear more letters. You may need to explain that there is another letter in *rocket* that sounds the same as *k,* and that the final part of the word *rocket* sounds like *it* but is actually spelled with a letter *e.* Eventually the whole word will appear in the boxes. This technique allows children to feel that they have spelled the word with some help from you, rather than having simply been told the spelling.

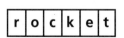

Encourage the children to keep on reading their sentences as they are writing them, so that they don't leave words out, or forget what they wanted to say. Remind them about the use of capital letters, full stops and so on, and make sure they read their writing through carefully when they have finished, to check that it makes sense and to see if they can improve the spelling and punctuation.

Supporting spelling (Look–Say –Cover–Write–Check)

If you train children to learn a new word by this method every time they want to remember a spelling, they will nearly always be successful.

Have a good LOOK at the word and its shape.
SAY the word and spell out the letters.
COVER the word so that you can't copy it.
WRITE the word down.
CHECK to see if it's right.

The children should repeat the process as often as necessary until they get the word right three times running. Even if the spelling is forgotten later, they will probably have most of the letters right, and relearning will be much quicker the second time.

One reason this method works is because it uses three different ways to learn the same thing.

You use your:
- **eyes** to look at the word
- **ears** to hear the letter names as you say them
- **hand** to write the word, and get the feel of its pattern and shape.

This gives the brain several chances to store the word in the memory.

It can help children's handwriting development as well as their spelling if they write the words in joined writing, so that they are learning the spelling patterns as a continuous movement.

Making spelling resources

Some of the activities in this book refer to the use of a word wheel and flick book. These can be made very easily and children really do enjoy using them.

Making a word wheel to learn spelling patterns

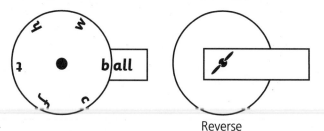

Reverse

Use a butterfly fastener in the centre of the card.

Making a flick book to learn spelling patterns

Staple here.

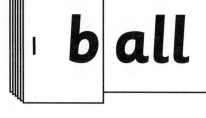

Write a different letter on each small piece of paper to make words, such as *wall, fall, tall* and so on.

Week 1 Mr Gumpy's Outing

by John Burningham

Introduction

This well-loved story about Mr Gumpy has been entertaining children for 30 years. John Burningham's delightful watercolour illustrations have made the story a classic picture book. Mr Gumpy is hoping for a peaceful boat ride. But the children and animals he takes along forget to behave themselves, resulting in no end of squabbling, chasing, teasing and flapping. Needless to say, they all end up in the river. The long-suffering Mr Gumpy bears no grudges, however, and provides tea and the promise of another outing.

The story consists largely of dialogue, providing the opportunity for children to practise reading with expression. This structure, with its repeated injunction of *don't*, is one the children can use to write their own stories, using the writing frame on Day 5.

Week 1 Objectives

	Word level	Sentence level	Text level
Day 1 Reading	To learn new words from reading Y2 T1 (10)	To identify speech marks in reading, understand their purpose, use the term correctly Y2 T2 (6)	To use title, cover and pictures to predict content Y1 T3 (7) To use phonological, contextual, grammatical and graphic knowledge Y1 & Y2 (2)
Day 2 Reading Comprehension		To predict from the text Y2 T2 (1)	To make sense of what they read Y1 & Y2 (2)
Day 3 High-frequency words Spelling by analogy	To read on sight and spell high-frequency words from List 1 Y1 & Y2 To recognise words by common spelling patterns Y1 T3 (5)		
Day 4 Phonological awareness *-ing* and *-ed*	To practise ability to hear initial phonemes *ch, sh* Y1 T2 (3) To investigate and learn spellings of verbs with *-ed* and *-ing* endings (past and present tense) Y1 T3 (6)		
Day 5 Writing			To write stories using simple settings, based on reading Y1 T3 (14)
Homework task 1 Jumbled sentences		To reorder sentences Y1 T3 (4)	
Homework task 2 Rhyming words	To know the common spelling pattern for long vowel phoneme *oa* Y1 T3 (1)		

Reading

Introducing the story

Look at the cover and draw the children's attention to the:

- title
- author/illustrator.

Discuss what kind of outing the story will be about. Who is going with Mr Gumpy? Look through the story together, as far as the page showing the goat, encouraging the children to predict what will happen before you turn each page.

Ask each child to say how they think the story will end. Continue looking through the story to see if anyone correctly guessed the ending.

Shared reading

Read the text to the children, encouraging them to join in with as much of it as they can manage. The children should be following the text carefully in their individual copies as they read. Alternatively, you could use a Big Book, if one is available.

Ask the children to point to the speech marks on one page. Make sure they understand that these indicate the words spoken by one of the characters. (You could explain them as 'talking marks'.)

Choose pairs of children to read a page containing dialogue, one child reading Mr Gumpy's words, the other reading the words of the second character.

Ask the children to find examples of question marks and to read aloud the questions asked by some of the animals in the story, with appropriate expression.

Make sure the children have understood the vocabulary *squabble, tease, bleating, calf* and *trample*.

Reading

Re-read the text all the way through, with individual children reading some pages. (You could allow a less able reader to read in a pair with a more confident child.)

Ask the children to find and read examples of words that sound like their meaning, for example *quack, sploosh.* (The correct term for these words is 'onomatopoeic'. If the teacher prefers the children not to use this term yet, you could refer to them as 'noisy words'.)

Comprehension

Story quiz (oral answers)

1. What did Mr Gumpy tell the children not to do?
A. *Squabble.*
2. Who chased the rabbit?
A. *The cat.*
3. Where did the story take place?
A. *On the river.*
4. What happened to the boat?
A. *It tipped.*
5. Who said, 'Can you make room for me?'
A. *The calf.*

Story quiz (written answers)

The children could work individually or in pairs, discussing their answers, taking turns to write and helping each other with spelling.
1. Did Mr Gumpy have a boat or a car?
A. *A boat.*
2. What did Mr Gumpy tell the chickens not to do?
A. *Flap.*
3. Who mucked about?
A. *The pig.*
4. How did they all get to the bank?
A. *Swam.*
5. Did they have tea in the boat?
A. *No.*

Sight vocabulary

said

Ask the children to find *said* in the text. Write *said* on a dry-wipe board, with the children spelling the letter names as you write. Ask the children to look closely at the word, count the letters and look for tall letters.

Say the word and spell the letter names aloud together.

In pairs, taking turns, each child can practise tracing the word on their partner's back while saying the letter names aloud.

The children should now try to write the word *said* from memory, using the Look–Say–Cover–Write–Check method (see page 6). They could also write the word in their spelling books to take home for revision.

Phonological awareness

Word beginnings game

Ask the children to think of other words that begin like *said*, with the letter *s*. Make sure they all know the phoneme (sound) for the letter.

Brainstorm words starting with *s*, then compose a sentence beginning *On a sunny Saturday Sally went swimming…* containing as many words as possible starting with *s*.

Spelling by analogy

Spelling pattern: -oat

Ask the children to find the word *boat* in the story. Make sure they can all spell *boat*, using the Look–Say–Cover–Write–Check method (see page 6).

• Which animal in the story rhymes with *boat*? (*Goat*.)
• Can they suggest rhyming words, for example *float, coat*?

Silly words game

Write the following headings on a dry-wipe board: *Real words* and *Silly words*. Ask the children to choose any consonant and put it in front of *-oat*, then write it under the correct heading. Add more words ending in *-oat* and read the lists of rhyming words together.

Dictate the following sentence for the children to write. (Decide if you want them to have the rhyming word list for reference.)

*Did the **goat float** in a **boat**?*

Ask the children to check their sentences, then underline the *-oat* words.

They could make word wheels or flick books with the spelling pattern to take home (see page 6).

Phonological awareness

Sheep and chickens game
(consonant digraphs *sh* and *ch*)

Ask the children to find the words *sheep* and *chickens* in the story and tell you how each word starts: *sh* and *ch*.

Now help them to think of other words beginning with *sh*, then with *ch*.

Divide the group into 'sheep' and 'chickens'. The 'sheep' should call out their name when you say a word starting with *sh*, and the 'chickens' should call out theirs if the word starts with *ch*.

chips	shopping	chair	cheese
ships	shell	shilling	chick
shine	shan't	check	chilly

Word endings *-ing* and *-ed*

Turn to the page where the children and animals on the boat start to misbehave. Can they find the word *kicked* and any other words on the page that end like *kicked*?

Write a list on the board of the words found by the children, for example *hopped, squabbled*. Make sure they recognise that all the words refer to actions – that is, verbs.

Ask them what the chickens are doing in the picture (flapping). Write the word *flapping* alongside *flapped* on your list.

Help the children to write on the board the appropriate words that end with *-ing* alongside the words that have the *-ed* ending. They could take turns to read the words, in pairs, for example *hopped, hopping*. Make sure they notice that only the ending of the word changes.

Mr Gumpy's Holiday

One day Mr Gumpy was going camping.
He got out his tent.
  "May I come with you?"
said the monkey.
  "Yes, if you don't chatter,"
said Mr Gumpy.

_____

_____

_____

_____

_____

_____

_____

_____

Shared or independent writing

Explain that the children are going to write a story called *Mr Gumpy's Holiday*. Mr Gumpy is going camping and can take three
friends. Before the children start to write, discuss the characters, events and the ending, and write key words on a dry-wipe board.

Jumbled words

Parents – please help your child to read through this Homework sheet to make sure they understand what to do.

The words in these sentences from *Mr Gumpy's Outing* have become mixed up. Can you write them in the right order?

1. went   boat.   Gumpy   Mr   his   in   out

2. come   I   May   Mr   please   Gumpy?

3. to   bank.   They   swam   all   the

4. home   tea.   for   Then   went   they

5. house   river.   by   Gumpy's   Mr   a   was

1. _____

   _____

2. _____

   _____

3. _____

   _____

4. _____

   _____

5. _____

   _____

Homework

Silly words

Parents – please help your child to read through this Homework sheet to make sure they understand what to do.

All the words below rhyme with **boat**, but some of them are not real words. Read the words first. Then write them in the correct list.

boat	goat	hoat	
poat	coat	gloat	float
sloat	moat	woat	

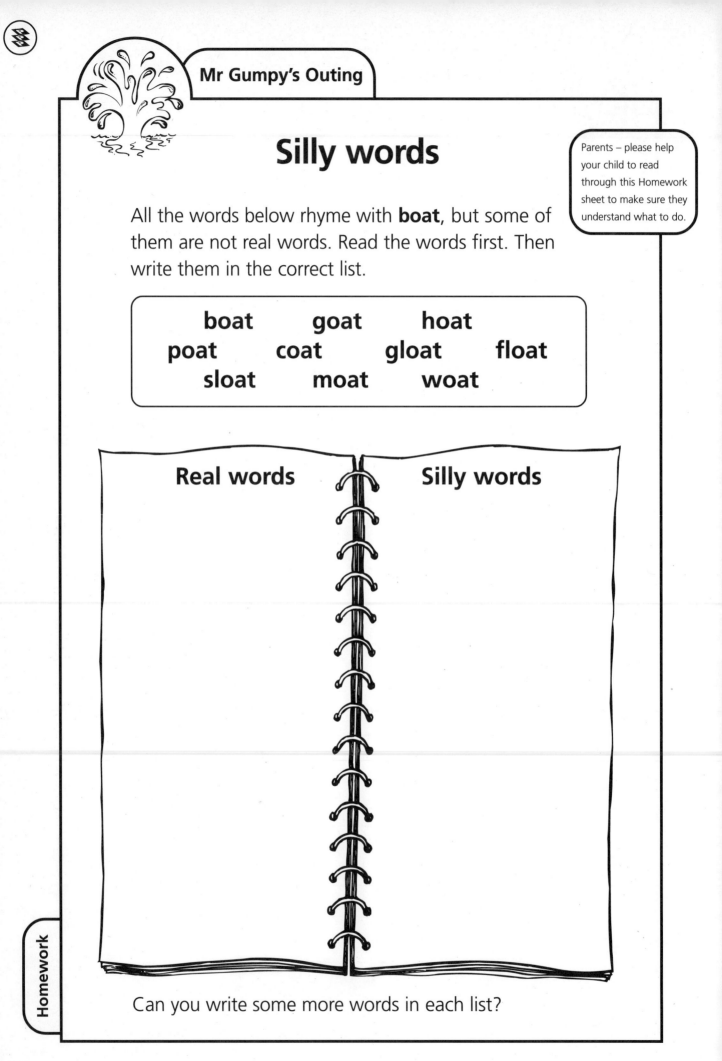

Real words   **Silly words**

Can you write some more words in each list?

Week 2   Titch
by Pat Hutchins

Introduction

This is the first of Pat Hutchins' stories about Titch, the little brother who suffers the same fate as the 'baby' in many families. Everything his older brother and sister have seems to be bigger and better than anything Titch has. Until, that is, the day they decide to do some gardening and give Titch the smallest thing they can find – a tiny seed. Soon the tables are turned, to Titch's delight, as his plant outgrows even his great big brother, Pete. The illustrations reflect the story beautifully, as the smug expressions of the big brother and sister turn eventually to dismay.

Week 2 Objectives

	Word level	Sentence level	Text level
Day 1 Reading	To learn new words from reading Y2 T1 (10)		To use title, cover and pictures to predict content Y1 T3 (7) To use phonological, contextual, grammatical and graphic knowledge Y1 & Y2 (2)
Day 2 Reading Sequencing Comprehension		To predict from the text Y2 T2 (1)	To make sense of what they read Y1 & Y2 (2) To retell stories and give the main points in sequence Y1 T3 (5)
Day 3 High-frequency words Spelling by analogy Phonological awareness	To read on sight and spell high-frequency words from List 1 Y1 & Y2 To recognise words by common spelling patterns Y1 T3 (5) To identify initial phonemes Y1 T2 (1)		
Day 4 Phonological awareness Capital letters	To discriminate words with initial consonant clusters Y1 T2 (3)	Revise knowledge about uses of capitalisation Y2 T1 (5)	
Day 5 Writing			To use story settings from reading for use in own writing Y2 T2 (13)
Homework task 1 Capital letters		To know common uses of capitalisation Y1 T3 (5)	
Homework task 2 Wordsearch	To read on sight and spell high-frequency words from List 1 Y1 & Y2		

Reading

Introducing the story
Look at the cover and draw the children's attention to the:
- title
- author.

Ask the children why there is only one name on the cover. (Pat Hutchins is both illustrator and author.) Discuss briefly what the story might be about.

Look through the book together, with the children telling the story from the pictures. Encourage them to predict what will happen on the next page as you go through it.

Discuss briefly which of the children is the youngest/oldest and so on in their own families. Which do they think is best to be?

Ask the children to find the names of the characters on a few pages (Pete, Mary and Titch). Make sure they understand why Titch has his nickname.

Shared reading
Read the whole story, with the children joining in with as much of the text as they can manage.

Check that they understand any words that might prove difficult, for example *tricycle, pinwheel, spade, saw*.

Make sure the children are following the text as they read, by pointing to the words in their copies. Alternatively, you could use a Big Book, if one is available.

Independent reading
Divide the group so that each child is allocated to either Mary, Pete or Titch. Re-read the text all the way through, with the 'Mary' children reading only the pages about Mary, and so on.

Comprehension

Retelling the story
Encourage the children to take turns saying one sentence each to tell the story in the correct sequence. If they are stuck, they could look at the pictures in the book for help.

Re-read the text all the way through, with individual children reading some pages. (You could pair a less able reader with a more confident child.)

Story quiz (oral answers)
1. What was Titch riding?
A. *A tricycle.*
2. Where did Titch put the seed?
A. *In the flowerpot.*
3. When did Mary and Pete stop looking pleased with themselves?
A. *When Titch's seed started to grow.*

4. Who had a hammer?
A. *Mary.*
5. Why was Titch happy at the end?
A. *Because he finally had something bigger than Mary and Pete.*

Story quiz (written answers)
The children could work individually or in pairs, discussing their answers, taking turns to write and helping each other with spelling.
1. What was Titch's brother called?
A. *Pete.*
2. Who had a flowerpot?
A. *Mary.*
3. Who was the youngest in the family?
A. *Titch.*
4. What did Pete and Mary ride?
A. *Bikes.*
5. Missing word: Mary had a _____ bike.
A. *Big.*

Week 2 Titch
Day 1

Week 2 Titch
Day 2

Sight vocabulary

little

Ask the children to find *little* in the text. Write *little* on a dry-wipe board, with the children spelling the letter names as you write.

Ask the children to look closely at the word, count the letters and look for tall letters. Can they tell you which small word they can see hiding inside *little*? *(It.)*

The children should now try to write the word *little* from memory, using the Look–Say–Cover–Write–Check method (see page 6). They could also write the word in their spelling books to take home for revision.

Phonological awareness

Word beginnings game

Ask the children to think of other words that begin like *little*, with the letter *l*. Make sure they all know the phoneme (sound) for the letter.

Brainstorm words starting with *l*, then compose a sentence beginning *Little Lucy liked licking lollipops and...* containing as many words as possible starting with *l*.

Spelling by analogy

Spelling pattern: -ig

Ask the children to find the word *big* in the story. Make sure they can all spell *big*, using the Look–Say–Cover–Write–Check method (see page 6).

Ask the children to suggest rhyming words, for example *dig, pig, fig*.

Silly words game

Write the following headings on a dry-wipe board: *real words* and *silly words*. Ask the children to choose any consonant and put it in front of *-ig*, then write it under the correct heading. Add more words ending in *-ig* and read the lists of rhyming words together.

Dictate the following sentence for the children to write. (Decide if you want them to have the rhyming word list for reference.)

*The **big pig** did a **jig**.*

Ask the children to check their sentences, then underline the *-ig* words.

They could make word wheels or flick books with the spelling pattern to take home (see page 6).

Resources for Group Time

Phonological awareness

Consonant clusters

Ask the children to find *flowerpot* (*Mary had a fat flowerpot*) and to notice the two letters at the start of the word: *fl*.

Make sure they can blend the *f* and *l* to produce *fl*. Help them to think of a few more words beginning with *fl*.

Now ask them to find the difference at the beginning of *fat* and *flowerpot*. (There is no *l* after the *f* in *fat*.) Ask each child to say a word beginning with *f* (but not *fl*).

Ask the children to call out 'flowerpots' when they hear a word starting with *fl*, as you read the following words: *flat, feet, flowerpot, fish, fingers, fleet, fancy, flash, fortune, flag, flick, frog.*

Capital letters

Ask the children to find the names of the characters in the story at least three times. What do they notice about the first letter of each name? (It has a capital letter.)

Help them to think of other names that start with *P, M* or *T*. They should write a list of names, starting with the names of the children in the group, continuing with the names from the story and family or friends' names. Make sure that they begin each one with a capital letter.

Resources for Group Time

Titch again

Pete had a great big ball
and Mary had a big ball.
Titch had a _____

_____

Pete had a _____

_____

and Mary had a _____

_____

Titch had a _____

_____

_____

_____

_____

_____

_____

Independent writing

Explain to the children that they are going to write another story about Titch. Discuss the pictures and write a list of key words together before they start writing.

Titch

Parents – please help your child to read through this Homework sheet to make sure they understand what to do.

Write the names in the sentences. Don't forget the capital letters.

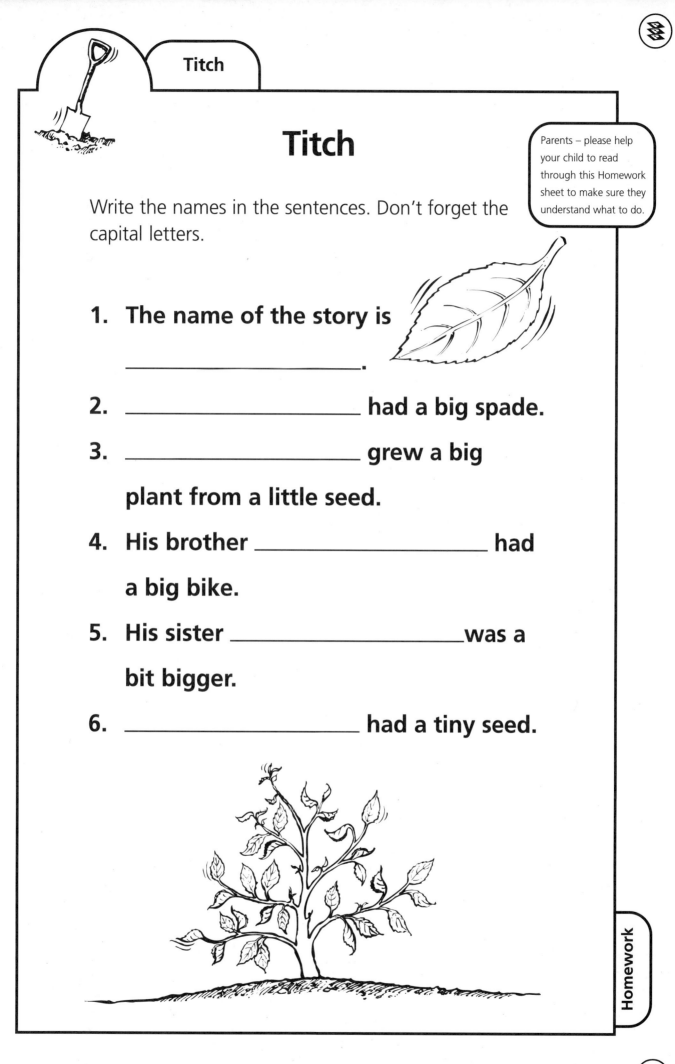

1. **The name of the story is** _____.

2. _____ **had a big spade.**

3. _____ **grew a big plant from a little seed.**

4. **His brother** _____ **had a big bike.**

5. **His sister** _____ **was a bit bigger.**

6. _____ **had a tiny seed.**

Wordsearch

Parents – please help your child to read through this Homework sheet to make sure they understand what to do.

Find each of these words in the wordsearch square. Colour in each word in the square as you find it.

Titch	Pete	Mary
big	little	bigger
seed	tiny	had

g	P	e	t	e	s	h
t	i	n	y	h	a	d
l	i	t	t	l	e	k
M	a	r	y	b	i	g
T	i	t	c	h	h	j
g	s	e	e	d	h	t
v	b	i	g	g	e	r

Can you read all the words?

Week 3 The Pig in the Pond

by Martin Waddell, illustrated by Jill Barton

Introduction

This is the joyous story of the poor pig who sits by Farmer Neligan's pond, on the hottest and driest of days, envying the ducks and geese as they honk, quack and splash in the water. Finally, despite the fact that 'pigs don't swim', she can stand the heat no longer and jumps in the pond and splashes to her heart's content. Her enjoyment is infectious and all the animals dive into the water, until Neligan reappears and joins them in the pond himself.

There are plenty of opportunities for children to read with expression in the story, using the punctuation as they do so, and to enjoy the wonderfully onomatopoeic words.

Week 3 Objectives

	Word level	Sentence level	Text level
Day 1 Reading	To learn new words from reading Y2 T1 (10)		To use title, cover and pictures to predict content Y1 T3 (7) To use phonological, contextual, grammatical and graphic knowledge Y1 & Y2 (2)
Day 2 Reading Comprehension		To predict from the text Y2 T2 (1) To take account of exclamation marks in reading aloud with appropriate expression Y2 T1 (3)	To make sense of what they read Y1 & Y2 (2)
Day 3 High-frequency words Spelling by analogy	To read on sight and spell high-frequency words from List 1 Y1 & Y2 To recognise words by common spelling patterns Y1 T3 (5) To identify initial phonemes Y1 T2 (1)		
Day 4 Phonological awareness Speech marks	To discriminate words with initial consonant clusters Y1 T2 (3)	To identify speech marks in reading Y2 T2 (6)	
Day 5 Writing			To apply phonological knowledge and sight vocabulary to spell Y1 T3 (12)
Homework task 1 Comprehension			To make sense of what they read Y1 & Y2 (2)
Homework task 2 Wordsearch	To read on sight and spell high-frequency words from List 1 Y1 & Y2		

Reading

Introducing the story

Look at the cover and draw the children's attention to the:

- title
- author
- illustrator.

Discuss briefly what the story might be about. Look through the book together, with the children telling the story from the pictures. Encourage them to predict what will happen on the next page.

Make the most of the animal noises: *splash, sploosh, honked, quacked, gulped.*

Shared reading

Read the whole story, with the children joining in with as much of the text as they can manage, particularly the repeated phrases and animal noises. Check that they understand any new vocabulary, for example *trotters, gulped, gasped.*

Make sure the children are following the text carefully in their individual copies as they read. Alternatively, you could use a Big Book, if one is available.

Reading

Re-read the text all the way through, with individual children reading some pages. (You could allow a less able reader to read in a pair with a more confident child).

Ask half the group to find all the onomatopoeic (or 'noisy') words for animal sounds, for example *quack, honk*, and the other half to find the onomatopoeic words for watery sounds.

Comprehension

Story quiz (oral answers)

1. Name two water birds in the story.
A. *Ducks and geese.*
2. Where are a pig's trotters?
A. *At the end of its legs.*
3. What did the pig do to her tail?
A. *Twirled it.*
4. What did all the animals shout?
A. *'The pig's in the pond!'*
5. Who is Neligan?
A. *The farmer.*

Story quiz (written answers)

The children could work individually or in pairs, discussing their answers, taking turns to write and helping each other with spelling.
1. What did Neligan take off first?
A. *His hat.*
2. Who went 'Quack!'?
A. *The ducks.*
3. How did Neligan travel?
A. *On his cart.*
4. Missing word: She didn't go in, because pigs don't _____.
A. *Swim.*
5. Describe the weather in the story.
A. *Hot and sunny.*

Sight vocabulary

went

Ask the children to find *went* in the text. Write *went* on a dry-wipe board, with the children spelling the letter names as you write.

Ask the children to look closely at the word, count the letters and look for tall letters.

The children should now try to write the word *went* from memory, using the Look–Say–Cover–Write–Check method (see page 6). They could also write the word in their spelling books to take home for revision.

Phonological awareness

Word beginnings game

Ask the children to think of other words that begin like *went*, with the letter *w*. Make sure they all know the phoneme (sound) for the letter.

Encourage them to think of 'question words' that begin with *w: what, where, when* and so on.

Brainstorm words starting with *w*, then compose a sentence beginning *One wet Wednesday, Wayne was…* containing as many words as possible starting with *w*.

Spelling by analogy

Spelling pattern: -un

Ask the children to find the word *sun* in the story. Make sure they can all spell *sun,* using the Look–Say–Cover–Write–Check method (see page 6).

Ask the children to suggest rhyming words, for example *fun, run, bun*.

Silly words game

Write the following headings on a dry-wipe board: *Real words* and *Silly words*. Ask the children to choose any consonant and put it in front of *-un*, then write it under the correct heading. Add more words ending in *-un* and read the lists of rhyming words together.

Dictate the following sentence for the children to write. (Decide if you want them to have the rhyming word list for reference.)

*Is it **fun** to **run** in the **sun**?*

Ask the children to check their sentences, then underline the *-un* words.

They could make word wheels or flick books with the spelling pattern to take home (see page 6).

Week 3 **The Pig in the Pond**

Day 3

Phonological awareness

Splashers and swimmers game (consonant clusters sp and sw)

Ask the children to find the words *splash* and *swim* in the story and tell you the first two letters of each word: *sp* and *sw*.

Now help them to think of other words beginning with *sp*, then with *sw*.

Divide the group into 'splashers' and 'swimmers'. The 'splashers' should call out their name when you say a word starting with *sp*, and the 'swimmers' should call out theirs if the word starts with *sw*.

swan	sploosh	swish	swing
speak	spare	spot	sparrow
swore	swap	spelling	swam

Speech marks

Using the pages with the repeated sentence *'The pig's in the pond!'*, ask the children how readers know when someone is talking in a story.

Make sure they notice the 'talking marks' and know the correct term: *speech marks*. You could help them to remember them as '66 and 99' (the shape of the marks).

Read these pages together with appropriate expression, as if the creatures were really talking (or shouting!).

Each child should choose a sentence or phrase in speech marks from the story and carefully copy it, placing the speech marks correctly.

Week 3 **The Pig in the Pond**

Day 4

Splash!

Independent writing

Explain to the children that they are going to write what they think the animals in the story were saying. They can use some of the words from the text, but they should also add ideas of their own. Discuss a few suggestions before they start writing.

Yes or no?

Parents – please help your child to read through this Homework sheet to make sure they understand what to do.

Try to remember the story of *The Pig in the Pond*.
Answer yes or no to each question.

1. **The ducks went "Quack!"**

2. **Neligan went in his car.**

3. **Pigs can swim.**

4. **They all said, "The pig's in the water."**

5. **The pig went "Quack!"**

6. **Neligan did not take off his hat.**

Wordsearch

Parents – please help your child to read through this Homework sheet to make sure they understand what to do.

Find each of these words in the wordsearch square.
Colour in each word in the square as you find it.

splash	pig	pond
ducks	on	water
went	out	and

p	d	u	c	k	s	h
o	u	t	f	a	n	d
s	w	e	n	t	o	n
w	a	t	e	r	a	t
s	p	l	a	s	h	l
l	p	i	g	k	p	x
y	p	o	n	d	v	p

Can you read all the words?

Week 4 Traditional rhymes

'Counting magpies', Oliver Twist' and 'Anna Elise'

Introduction

The three poems selected for this poetry section are all traditional rhyming verses that have been heard in playgrounds for many years. Two of the poems ('Counting magpies' and 'Oliver Twist') are chants based on counting, and two are action verses ('Anna Elise' and 'Oliver Twist'). Although nowadays children are perhaps more likely to be singing the lyrics to the latest chart music or television theme tunes, they still enjoy the catchy rhythms and memorable rhymes of long-established verses. The strong rhythms of traditional poems often grew in response to a playtime activity, such as clapping games or skipping, and the beat of the verse is one that demands an active response. It might be appropriate to begin the lesson in the playground! The writing activity on Day 5 could produce rhymes that can be added to the playground repertoire.

Week 4 Objectives

	Word level	Sentence level	Text level
Day 1 Reading		To read aloud with intonation and expression Y2 T2 (2)	To identify and discuss favourite poems Y2 T2 (11)
Day 2 Comprehension			To make sense of what they read Y1 & Y2 (2)
Day 3 High-frequency words Spelling by analogy	To read on sight and spell high-frequency words from List 1 Y1 & Y2 To recognise words by common spelling patterns Y1 T3 (5)		
Day 4 Rhymes			To identify and discuss patterns of rhyme Y2 T2 (9)
Day 5 Writing			To use structures from poems as a basis for writing Y2 T2 (15)
Homework task 1 Cloze			To make sense of what they read Y1 & Y2 (2)
Homework task 2 Cloze		To predict from the text, read on, leave a gap and re-read Y2 T2 (1)	

Reading

Introducing the story

Look at the three traditional rhymes on photocopiable pages 43 and 44 with the children, and talk about the way the text is organised. Ask the children how they can tell whether the text in each section is a story, information text or a poem. Encourage them to say how they know. (The layout is in short lines.)

Tell the children the names of the poems.

Shared reading

The poems can be read in any order, so if any of the children know one of the poems, begin with that one. Read each poem to the children, encouraging them to join in as much as possible. Make sure the children are following the text as they read, by pointing to the words in their copies.

Check that they understand any words that might prove difficult, for example *rare, frail, pail.*

Re-read the first four lines of 'Anna Elise' together, listening for the rhymes.

Discuss any other number rhymes the children may know (for example, *One, two, buckle my shoe…* and *One two three four five, once I caught a fish alive…*)

Independent reading

Divide the children into two groups, and re-read 'Anna Elise', with each group reading two lines in turn.

Comprehension

Memory skills

Re-read the 'Counting magpies' poem together.

Now ask the children to turn over their copies of the poems. Read 'Counting magpies' aloud, pausing at the end of each line for the children to supply the missing word, for example *One for* _____*, two for* _____.

Re-read either 'Anna Elise' or 'Oliver Twist' in the same way.

'Anna Elise' quiz (oral answers)

1. What did the surprise do to Anna Elise?
A. *Played her a trick.*
2. Where did she jump first?
A. *On a chair.*
3. Why did she jump in a net?
A. *Because the pail was so wet.*
4. What sort of ball was it?
A. *A round one.*
5. Was the net a big one?
A. *No, it was small.*

'Oliver Twist' quiz (written answers)

The children could work individually or in pairs, discussing their answers, taking turns to write and helping each other with spelling.
1. What should you wiggle for number six?
A. *Your hips.*
2. When do you start again?
A. *Ten.*
3. Missing word: I _____ you a penny you can't do this.
A. *Bet.*
4. Yes or no? Number four, touch the door.
A. *No (floor).*
5. When do you tie your shoe?
A. *Two.*

Sight vocabulary

one

Ask the children to find *one* in the 'Oliver Twist' text. Write *one* on a dry-wipe board, with the children spelling the letter names as you write.

Ask the children to look closely at the word and count the letters. Can they tell you which small word they can see hiding inside *one*? *(On.)*

Say the word and spell the letter names aloud together.

In pairs, taking turns, each child can practise tracing the word on their partner's back while saying the letter names aloud.

The children should now try to write the word *one* from memory, using the Look–Say–Cover–Write–Check method (see page 6). They could also write the word in their spelling books to take home for revision.

Spelling by analogy

Spelling pattern: -et

Ask the children to find the word *net* in *Anna Elise*. Make sure they can all spell *net*, using the Look–Say–Cover–Write–Check method (see page 6).

Ask the children to suggest rhyming words, for example *bet, pet, wet*.

Silly words game

Write the following headings on a dry-wipe board: *Real words* and *Silly words*. Ask the children to choose any consonant and put it in front of *-et*, then write it under the correct heading. Add more words ending in *-et* and read the lists of rhyming words together.

Dictate either or both of the following sentences for the children to write. (Decide if you want them to have the rhyming word list for reference.)

*Did you **let** the **vet** see my **pet**?*
*I **bet** he **let** the **net get wet**.*

Ask the children to check their sentences, then underline the *-et* words.

They could make word wheels or flick books with the spelling pattern to take home (see page 6).

Rhymes

Ask the children to listen carefully for the rhymes as you read 'Counting magpies' together. Highlight or underline the rhymes, using coloured felt-tipped pens (*joy/buy, gold/told*).

Help the children to notice where the rhymes appear in this poem (at the end of every other line).

Read 'Anna Elise' together in the same way, listening for the rhymes and marking them in the text.

Ask the children how the patterns of rhyme are different in the two poems. (Each line in 'Anna Elise' ends with a rhyme.)

Read 'Oliver Twist' together, without marking the rhymes. Individually, or in pairs,

the children should read the poem again, marking the rhymes.

Discuss the different rhyming pattern for 'Oliver Twist'. (There is an internal rhyme rather than a final rhyme in each line.)

New rhymes

Encourage the children to think of new rhymes for some of the lines in 'Anna Elise'.

*The chair was so **red**,*
*She jumped on a **bed**.*
*The bed was so **high**,*
*She jumped in the **sky**.*
*The sky was so **blue**,*
*She jumped on her **shoe**.*

A playtime rhyme

This is the story of number one,

Playtime should be full of fun.

This is the story of number two,

_____

This is the story of number three,

_____

_____

_____

_____

_____

_____

_____

_____

_____

_____

When we get to number ten,

That is when we start again.

two
blue
shoe
glue
new

three
tree
see
me
knee

four
door
floor
more
pour

five
dive
alive
jive
hive

six
mix
sticks
fix
bricks

seven
heaven
Devon

eight
wait
mate
late
gate

nine
mine
fine
shine
wine

Shared or independent writing

Explain to the children that they are going to write their own number rhymes suitable for skipping or clapping at playtime. Help them to read the suggested rhymes for some of the numbers first.

Missing words

Parents – please help your child to read through this Homework sheet to make sure they understand what to do.

The numbers are missing from the poem. Find the correct words from the bottom of the page and write them in the spaces.

Oliver, Oliver, Oliver Twist

I bet you a penny you can't do this:

Number _____ , touch your tongue

Number _____ , tie your shoe

Number _____ , slap your knee

Number _____ , touch the floor

Number _____ , stay alive

Number _____ , wiggle your hips

Number _____ , jump to heaven

Number _____ , bang the gate

Number _____ , walk the line

Number _____ , start again.

	three	six	one	
four		two	five	eight
	ten	nine	seven	

Rhymes

Choose the rhyming words to fit the poem.

Anna Elise,

She jumped with surprise.

The surprise was so _____,   slick   quick   fat

It played her a trick.

The trick was so rare,

She jumped on a _____.   bed   chair   bear

The chair was so frail,

She jumped in a _____.   bucket   pail   sail

The pail was so wet,

She jumped in a _____.   pet   net   pond

The net was so _____,   big   small   little

She jumped on the ball.

The ball was so round,

She jumped on the ground.

And ever since then, she's been turning

_____.   up   around   sound

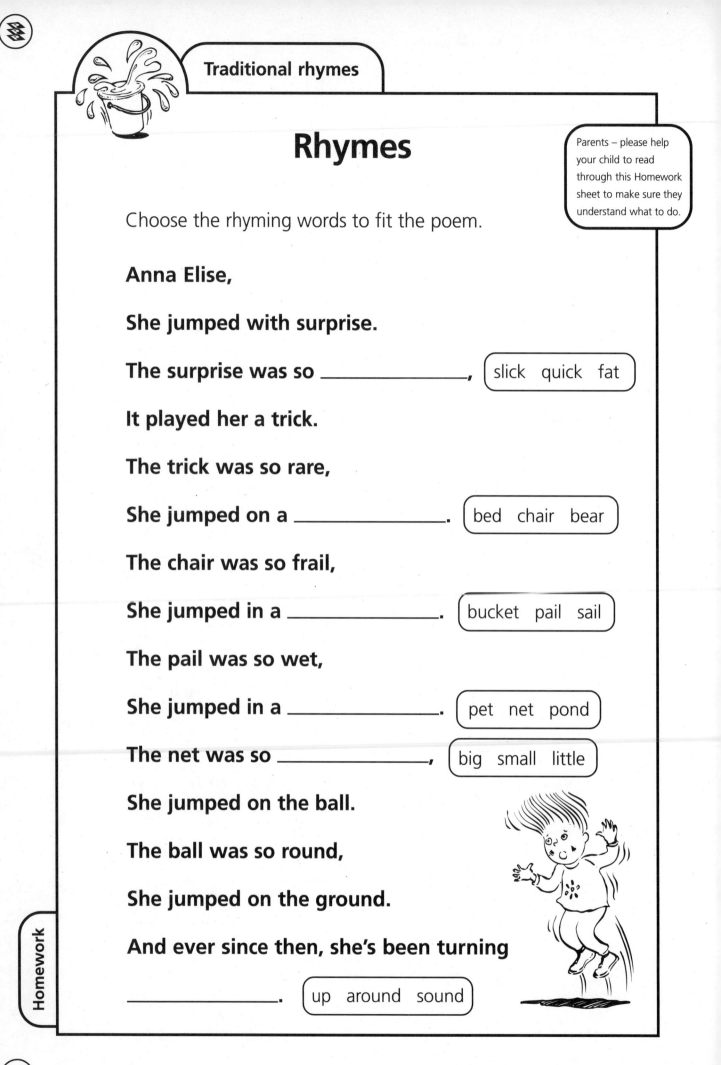

Week 5 Guess What I'll Be

by Anni Axworthy

Introduction

This non-fiction text, comprising extracts taken from *Guess What I'll Be* (Walker Books), introduces readers to the transformations that occur in nature, when creatures develop from their infant to adult stages. As the children read about the 'babies' (tadpole, chick, caterpillar and grub) they are encouraged to predict what each will become as it grows up. Turning the cards over reveals the adult creatures. Although children see this as a kind of game, it actually involves them in several important reading processes: thinking as they read, decision-making, using evidence on which to base their predictions and deductive reasoning.

Week 5 Objectives

	Word level	Sentence level	Text level
Day 1 Reading	To learn new words from reading Y2 T1 (10)	To expect reading to make sense and check if it does not Y1 T2 (1)	To note differing features of non-fiction Y1 T2 (17) To scan a text to find key words and phrases Y2 T3 (16)
Day 2 Reading Comprehension		To predict from the text Y2 T2 (1)	To make sense of what they read Y1 & Y2 (2) To make simple notes (key words) to use in own writing Y2 T3 (19)
Day 3 High-frequency words Spelling by analogy	To read on sight and spell high-frequency words from List 1 Y1 & Y2 To recognise words by common spelling patterns Y1 T3 (5)		
Day 4 Phonological awareness Sequencing	To discriminate words with initial consonant clusters Y1 T2 (3)		To make sense of what they read Y1 & Y2 (2)
Day 5 Writing			To write non-fiction texts using text read as model Y2 T3 (20)
Homework task 1 Jumbled sentences			To make sense of what they read Y1 & Y2 (2)
Homework task 2 Matching captions			To use the language and features of non-fiction texts (captions) Y1 T3 (21)

Reading

Before reading

Make copies of photocopiable pages 45 and 46 (enough for one set of cards for each child) and cut out the sections. Fold over each section and paste the sides together to make four cards. Give each child four different cards (with the sides showing the adult creatures face down). Do not allow the children to turn over the cards, or the surprise element will be lost.

Write the words *What will I be?* on a dry-wipe board and read them together. Explain to the children that when they have read the text on the first side of the card, they will have to guess what the creature is.

Make sure they all understand that this is a non-fiction or information text. Ask them what the difference is between non-fiction and fiction. (Fiction refers to stories and is not necessarily true, non-fiction is about facts and things which do happen or are true.)

Introducing the text

Look at the cards (first side only) with the children, and encourage them to discuss what they can see. Help them to find the words *tadpole, chick, caterpillar* and *grub.* Check that they understand each of the words, from the pictures.

Shared reading

Take the card about the tadpole and read the first part of the text to the children. Encourage them to join in with as much of the text as they can manage. The children should be following the text as they read, by pointing to the words on their card.

Ask the children what they think will be on the reverse side of the card. Let them look to see if they were correct, before reading the words *I'll be a frog!* with you.

Do the same with the other three cards: chick, caterpillar and grub.

After reading

Discuss with the children other animals whose babies are called:
- chicks (all birds, as well as hens)
- grubs (insects)
- tadpoles (toads)
- caterpillars (moths).

Resources for Group Time

✂

Reading

Read the text on all the cards again, with children taking turns to read text for different creatures. As you read, help the children to highlight or underline the key words about each creature, for example *tadpole; webby feet, big bulging eyes; eat beetles, flies and worms; frog.*

Comprehension

Quiz (oral answers)
1. What do frogs eat?
A. *Beetles, flies and worms.*
2. What is a baby flamingo called?
A. *A chick.*
3. Butterflies have wings and antennae. What are antennae?
A. *Long wavy feelers.*
4. What does a caterpillar become?
A. *A butterfly.*

5. What do bees make?
A. *Honey.*

Quiz (written answers)
The children could work individually or in pairs, discussing their answers, taking turns to write and helping each other with spelling.
1. Yes or no? Grubs can make honey.
A. *No.*
2. What does a tadpole become?
A. *A frog.*
3. What can a butterfly do that a caterpillar can't?
A. *Fly.*
4. How many legs has a bee?
A. *Six.*
5. What colour is a flamingo?
A. *Pink.*

Resources for Group Time

Resources for Group Time
Support for Struggling Readers

Sight vocabulary

will

Ask the children to find *will* on the cards. Write *will* on a dry-wipe board, with the children spelling the letter names as you write. Ask the children to look closely at the word, count the letters and look for tall letters.

Say the word and spell the letter names aloud together.

In pairs, taking turns, each child can practise tracing the word on their partner's back while saying the letter names aloud together.

The children should now try to write the word *will* from memory, using the Look–Say–Cover–Write–Check method (see page 6).

Make sure they are noticing the difference between the letters *i* and *l*. They could also write the word in their spelling books to take home for revision.

Spelling by analogy

Spelling pattern: -ill

Ask the children to suggest words that rhyme with *will*, for example *bill, still, till, fill, hill, pill, spill, chill*. They should then write them in a list on a dry-wipe board (or you can write the words for them). Read the list of rhyming words together.

Dictate either or both of the following sentences for the children to write. (Decide if you want them to have the rhyming word list for reference.)

*I was **ill**, so I had a **pill**.*
***Bill** went up the **hill**.*

Ask the children to check their sentences, then underline the *-ill* words.

They could make word wheels or flick books with the spelling pattern to take home (see page 6).

Resources for Group Time

Phonological awareness

Frogs and flamingoes game (consonant clusters)

Ask the children to find the words *frog* and *flamingo* on the cards and tell you how each word starts: *fr* and *fl*. Ensure the children can hear the difference between *fl* and *fr*.

Help the children to think of other words beginning with *fl*, then with *fr*.

Divide the group into 'frogs' and 'flamingoes'. The 'frogs' should call out their name when you say a word from the following list starting with *fr*, and the 'flamingoes' should call out theirs if the word starts with *fl*.

flash	*frying*	*fleet*	*flick*
frown	*fly*	*France*	*friend*
flapping	*flounce*	*frank*	*flapjack*

Sequencing words

Prepare for this activity by writing this sentence about a frog on a strip of card or paper: *One day I'll eat beetles, flies and worms.* Help the children to read the sentence.

Cut the sentence into separate words and mix them up. Help the children to put the words from the cut-up sentence into order, reading it to make sure it is correct.

Remove a word from the sentence and close the gap, while the children have their eyes closed. Encourage them to re-read the sentence to find the missing word.

Provide strips of paper for the children to write sentences on. Working in pairs, the children should choose a sentence from one of their cards and read it carefully. They should copy their sentence onto their strip of paper, cut out each word, jumble the words, then reassemble the sentence.

Taking turns, each child should hide one word from their sentence, while their partner's eyes are closed. The partner can then try to work out the missing word.

Resources for Group Time

What will I be?

This is me. I'm called a puppy.

One day I will _____

_____

This is me. I'm called a duckling.

One day I will _____

_____

This is me. I'm called a cub.

One day I will _____

_____

This is me. I'm called a lamb.

One day I will _____

_____

Writing composition

Look with the children at the illustrations above. Help them to write their own text about the animals, completing the sentence *One day I will…* They could write the answers on the back of the sheet. (Remind them about capital letters and full stops.)

Jumbled sentences

Parents – please help your child to read through this Homework sheet to make sure they understand what to do.

The words in these sentences are jumbled. Can you write them in the correct order?

1. grow   Tadpoles   frogs.   into

_____

2. pink   have   feathers.   Flamingoes

_____

_____

3. have   wings.   big   Butterflies   colourful

_____

_____

4. Frogs   eyes   have   feet.   and   big   webby

_____

_____

5. legs.   Bees   six   have

_____

Missing words

Find the correct name and write it under each creature.

chick   tadpole   caterpillar   grub

frog   bee   butterfly   flamingo

Week 6 — How to look after guinea pigs

Introduction

Children need to become familiar with the differences between fiction and information texts, and to learn how to approach non-fiction. This information text introduces children to the practical, everyday aspects of caring for a pet guinea pig. The use of some specific vocabulary (for example, *hutch*) and words which are more difficult to read (for example, *vegetables*) is unavoidable in non-fiction texts. In order to make it accessible to Level 1/2 readers, much of the text is in the form of captions, so that the illustrations can fully support the words. The KWL grid (Day 1) and the writing frame (Day 5) provide children with opportunities to revise and practise the necessary skills for tackling non-fiction.

Week 6 Objectives

	Word level	Sentence level	Text level
Day 1 Reading	To learn new words from reading Y2 T1 (10)		To understand the distinction between fact and fiction Y2 T3 (13) To identify questions and use text to find answers Y1 T3 (19)
Day 2 Reading Comprehension		To predict from the text Y2 T2 (1)	To make simple notes (key words) to use in own writing Y2 T3 (19)
Day 3 High-frequency words Spelling by analogy	To read on sight and spell high-frequency words from List 1 Y1 & Y2 To recognise words by common spelling patterns Y1 T3 (5)		
Day 4 Questions Syllables	To discriminate syllables in words Y2 T2 (5)	To turn statements into questions Y2 T3 (6)	
Day 5 Writing		To learn a range of words to open questions and to add question marks Y2 T3 (6)	To write own questions and to record answers Y1 T3 (22)
Homework task 1 Comprehension			To make sense of what they read Y1 & Y2 (2)
Homework task 2 Questions		To add question marks to questions Y1 T3 (7)	

Reading

Before reading

Before looking at the text on photocopiable pages 47 and 48, begin the KWL grid.

K = Things we **k**now
W = Things we **w**ant to know
L = Things we **l**earned

Things we **k**now	Things we **w**ant to know	Things we **l**earned

You will need to make a large grid, so that the whole group is able to see it.

Read the heading of the first column (Things we **k**now). Ask: 'What do you already know about guinea pigs?' and write down two or three suggestions. (This can be very simple, for example *Guinea pigs have fur*.)

Read the heading of the middle column (Things we **w**ant to know). Help the children to think of a few questions, and write them in this column.

Give each child a copy of the photocopiable sheets and read the title together: *How to look after guinea pigs.* Make sure they all understand that this is an information (or non-fiction) text. Ask them how it is different from a story. (Non-fiction is about facts and things which really happen or are true.)

Introducing the text

Look through the illustrations and encourage the children to discuss what they can see. Help them to find the following words:

guinea pigs   hutch   vegetables

Encourage the children to understand the meaning of these words from the illustrations.

Shared reading

Read the text to the children, encouraging them to join in with as much of it as they can manage. They should be following the text in their copies carefully as they read.

After reading

The children can make suggestions for information to write in the third column of the KWL grid (Things we **l**earned). They may not have found the answers to their earlier questions, and so could be encouraged to find other books about guinea pigs, or enlist help in searching Internet sites about guinea pigs, at another time.

Reading

Re-read the text together, perhaps with children taking turns to read different sections. As you read, help the children to highlight or underline the key words about looking after guinea pigs, for example:

food   water   hutch   straw

The children should write all the key words on a word web.

Comprehension

Quiz (oral answers)

1. Do guinea pigs like the rain?
A. *No.*
2. Where do pet guinea pigs live?
A. *In a hutch in the garden.*
3. What should you do to the hutch every week?
A. *Clean it and put in new straw.*
4. Name two things that guinea pigs like to eat.
A. *Dry food, fruit, vegetables and green leaves* (any two).
5. Where should the hutch be placed in the winter?
A. *In a shed or garage.*

Sight vocabulary

look

Ask the children to find *look* in the text. Write *look* on a dry-wipe board, with the children spelling the letter names as you write.

Ask the children to look closely at the word, count the letters and look for tall letters.

Say the word and spell the letter names aloud together.

The children should now try to write the word *look* from memory, using the Look–Say–Cover–Write–Check method (see page 6). They could also write the word in their spelling books to take home for revision.

Spelling by analogy

Spelling pattern: *-ook*

Ask the children to suggest rhyming words for *look*, for example *book, cook, hook, shook, took*.

Silly words game

Write the following headings on a dry-wipe board: *Real words* and *Silly words*. Ask the children to choose any consonant and put it in front of *-ook*, then write it under the correct heading. Add more words ending in *-ook* and read the lists of rhyming words together.

Dictate the following sentence for the children to write. (Decide if you want them to have the rhyming word list for reference.)

*The **cook took** a **look** at the **book**.*

Ask the children to check their sentences, then underline the *-ook* words.

They could make word wheels or flick books with the spelling pattern to take home (see page 6).

Questions

Ask the children to find the heading *How to look after guinea pigs*. Help them to think of a way to turn this phrase into a question (such as *How do you look after guinea pigs?*).

Write the question on a large dry-wipe board, without the question mark, and ask: 'What is missing?'

Find more sentences in the text and encourage the children to change them into questions, for example:

Guinea pigs make very good pets.
Do guinea pigs make very good pets?

Make sure the children understand when to use question marks. In turn, each child should find a sentence in the text, read it to the group, then change it into a question. The children could each write their own question.

Syllables

Ask the children to find the word *water*. As a group, clap the beats to count the syllables in the word (two claps: *wa/ter*). Do the same with *food* (one syllable) and *guinea pigs* (three syllables).

Think of some vegetables eaten by guinea pigs, for example *carrots, lettuce*. Say the name of each vegetable together, while clapping the syllables.

Questions about guinea pigs

1. **What** _____

   _____

2. **Where** _____

   _____

3. **What** _____

   _____

4. **How** _____

   _____

5. **When** _____

   _____

Day 5

Independent writing
Using the KWL grid from Day 1 and the word web from Day 2, help the children to write a few questions about guinea pigs. (Remind them first about capital letters and question marks.) When completed, they could exchange sheets with another child in the group and try to answer each other's questions.

Yes or no?

Parents – please help your child to read through this Homework sheet to make sure they understand what to do.

How much can you remember about guinea pigs?
Answer yes or no.

1. **Guinea pigs like to run.**

2. **Guinea pigs like rain.**

3. **Guinea pigs like green leaves.**

4. **Guinea pigs drink milk.**

5. **Should you wash your hands after holding a guinea pig?**

6. **Guinea pigs eat meat.**

7. **Guinea pigs drink water.**

Homework

Questions

Parents – please help your child to read through this Homework sheet to make sure they understand what to do.

Some of these sentences are questions, but the question marks are missing. Spot which ones are questions and write in the question marks.

Do guinea pigs like to be cuddled

What do guinea pigs eat

Guinea pigs do not like the cold

I like guinea pigs

Where do guinea pigs live

Are guinea pigs pets

Guinea pigs need a place to run

Now write your own question about guinea pigs.

_____

_____

_____

Homework

Traditional rhymes

Oliver Twist

Oliver, Oliver, Oliver Twist

I bet you a penny you can't do this:

Number one, touch your tongue

Number two, tie your shoe

Number three, slap your knee

Number four, touch the floor

Number five, stay alive

Number six, wiggle your hips

Number seven, jump to heaven

Number eight, bang the gate

Number nine, walk the line

Number ten, start again.

Counting magpies

One for sorrow

Two for joy

Three for a girl

Four for a boy

Five for silver

Six for gold

Seven for a secret never to be told.

Anna Elise

Anna Elise,

She jumped with surprise.

The surprise was so quick,

It played her a trick.

The trick was so rare,

She jumped on a chair.

The chair was so frail,

She jumped in a pail.

The pail was so wet,

She jumped in a net.

The net was so small,

She jumped on a ball.

The ball was so round,

She jumped on the ground.

And ever since then, she's been

turning around.

What will I be?

This is me. I'm called a tadpole.

One day I'll have four webby feet, big bulging eyes and I'll eat beetles, flies and worms. What will I be?

I'll be a frog!

This is me. I'm called a chick.

One day I'll have two long skinny legs, bright pink feathers and a very large hooked beak. What will I be?

fold

I'll be a flamingo!

This is me. I'm called a caterpillar.

One day
I'll have long wavy
feelers called antennae,
and big colourful
wings, and I'll fly
from flower to flower.
What will I be?

I'll be a butterfly!

This is me. I'm called a grub.

One day I'll
have six busy
legs and a stripy
body, and I'll make
honey. What will I be?

I'll be a bee!

fold

How to look after guinea pigs

Guinea pigs make very good pets. They are easy to look after.

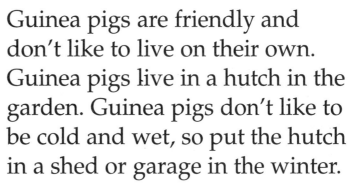

Guinea pigs are friendly and don't like to live on their own. Guinea pigs live in a hutch in the garden. Guinea pigs don't like to be cold and wet, so put the hutch in a shed or garage in the winter.

Clean out the hutch and put in new straw every week.

A safe place to run about, on the grass, is a good idea.

Give them food to eat and water to drink every day.

Guinea pigs like to eat dry food, fruit, vegetables and green leaves.

Guinea pigs like to be cuddled.

Brush your guinea pigs sometimes.

Pick up a guinea pig gently. Don't forget to wash your hands after you hold a guinea pig.

Anthology